How Women Sabotage Their Success in Business... According to Men

Michelle Bergquist

women lead
PUBLISHING™

Published by Women Lead Publishing

ISBN: 978-0-692-54007-7

PRINTED IN THE UNITED STATES OF AMERICA

First Edition: October, 2015

SPECIAL SALES
Books are available at special discounts for bulk purchases for
sales promotions or premiums. Special editions, including
personalized covers, excerpts of existing books, and corporate
imprints, can be created in large quantities for special needs.
For more information, write to Special Sales at Women
Lead Publishing, hello@womenleadpublishing.com.

To the Amazing Men I Interviewed

Thank you for your time and great insight. Your thoughts and advice have allowed me the opportunity to share your collective wisdom and ideas with professional women who seek to advance in business. Your feedback and ideas are priceless!

Thank you!

**To the Countless Women Seeking
to Advance in Business**

I hope you glean great value from the thoughts and ideas presented in this book.

Lead the way, ladies!

"If you allow your gender to be a factor in your success, then your success will be defined by your gender."

SVP / Technology Executive

*"Don't brand yourself as a woman.
Be judged by the content of your
character and abilities—not by sex."*

CEO / Commercial Properties

"When you come to a fork in the road, take the tough one."

VP / Risk Management

"It's easier to break through the glass ceiling when you use a baseball bat."

COO / Food Distribution

*"When emotion is taken out,
it doesn't come across as bitchy."*

President / PR Firm

Contents

Adapt, Don't Change
Be a Mirror
Don't Be a Guy
Stay True to Your Values
Aim Big
The Price of Perfection
Give Up Being Superwoman

My First Thoughts

"It is not the strongest of the species that survives, but the most adaptable."

Michelle and I first met in 2012. I was immediately impressed with her edgy, yet realistic approach to advocating for women in leadership roles and greatly appreciated her willingness to take on complex topics and initiatives that support the advancement of women. Michelle invited me to serve as a panelist for the upcoming Connected Women of Influence panel, "How Women Sabotage Their Success in Business….according to men." I was pleased to share my thoughts and insight on women and leadership.

As the parents of two daughters, my wife and I are personally concerned about how they enter the global economy and stand up for what they are worth. As a former naval officer and now private consultant in leadership development and training, I am even more concerned about having enough ethical and effective women and men leaders in the world. Most of my career in the military an engineering profession has been involved with recruiting, supporting and advocating for women in these very traditional male career fields and I know that challenges exist in other industries as well.

I predominantly teach leadership to all people, but I am frequently asked to speak on women leadership issues and challenges and Michelle's efforts through this excellent book highlight many of my own takeaways and insights.

To all aspiring and practicing leaders, it is about results and about adapting to the business environment and while you should certainly be yourself, you should also remember, "it's not about you," it's about the organization that you work for and the people that you lead.

Michael A. Giorgione
Rear Admiral, CEC, USN (Ret.)
Founder & Owner
LeadingLeaders LLC

I originally met Michelle Bergquist in 2001 and it was very apparent from the beginning that Michelle not only had a unique positive outlook on life, but a keen business sense that was supported by her never tiring work ethic. We became instant friends! Over the years we kept in touch and in 2012 I got a call from Michelle asking me to be on a man panel. She shared that she wanted my perspective among men in how women sabotage their success in business. My first reaction was, "Why not, should be fun."

I mentioned to a few male friends and colleagues that I was asked to serve on a man panel and was met with a strong reaction that ranged from, "Be careful my friend." to "Are you crazy?" The CEO of my then employer called me into his office and expressed a deep concern for me participating in such a panel and how it could have a negative impact on my standing in the community. He was also concerned in how it might reflect on the firm.

As time progressed and my male counterparts continued to try to convince me not to do the panel, I thought it was time to get serious and go in loaded with facts versus opinions. At the time I was asked to be on the panel, my daughter Vanessa was eight years old. From the day she was born I have wrestled with how I could be not only a good role model but more importantly how I could prepare her for the life ahead of her. I decided to get serious about the man panel and the contribution it could make to young women in the future.

I'm a firm believer in the value of market research and decided to do a little research of my own on the panel topic. I crafted a short email to over one hundred of my guy friends, colleagues and family. Much to my surprise, and pleasure, was the overwhelming response I received. Several of the emails started with comments like "Are you wearing body armor to the presentation? Another comment was "First, I would have respectfully declined this invitation. Second, now that you are knee deep in it, here are a few comments." Another friend said, "Interesting. Better you on this panel than me." One respondent concluded his email by saying, "Larry, don't use my name... I don't want to be sued." In general, the men that responded provided good solid advice for women that Michelle has integrated into this book with her own added in-depth research.

I currently sit on the board of an organization that holds an annual mentoring program for collage seniors. The program involves senior executives of brand name companies providing seniors with career advice. It was born out of the concept of providing young professionals guidance that we, as mentors, had wished we received when we were in our early 20's. My desire is that every woman will read this book, and use it to mentor young women as they begin their career.

In preparation for the man panel I was asked to complete a fun facts form and bio. One question that was asked was, "What's the most successful thing you've seen a woman do in business to get ahead?" My response was, "Be the best!" I believe that the focus for women should be on excellence in their performance and the job they do and not on gender. Ladies, be the best and your career will take care of itself.

Larry Sukay
Vice President
Patriot Risk & Insurance Services
San Diego, California

Introduction

My Mission to Find Answers

I wrote this book to find answers to two questions, "Why aren't more women leading the way in business? And, what's missing that prevents women from advancing to the top positions in business and industry?

Bold questions, right?

Women are smart. They're graduating from college at a rate equal to men, yet advancement for women still stops at the middle-management level.

As of the publishing of this book, here's the current state of women in the world of business. According to Catalyst, a nonprofit organization that conducts pioneering research on women and business, a 2015 report contained the following sad statistics:

1. Only 5% of Fortune 1000 firms are led by women.
2. 8% of top earners in the United States are women.
3. 17% of boardroom seats are represented by women.
4. Only 15% of executive officers are women.

So, I set out on a mission. My goal was to find an answer to what holds women back from advancing to top positions in business and industry. I set out to find the answer from a group of leaders who, to my knowledge, have never been asked what they think women do that sabotage their success in business. My mission: ask men.

A Little History

In 2010, the professional women's association I co-founded launched a series of panels designed to bring the best and brightest women leaders together to interact among peers, share business experiences and learn from one another's successes. We came up with the panel concept because our members asked to hear a variety of viewpoints relating to business and advancement.

In 2011, one of our members said, "Wouldn't it be great to hear from men on what we need to do to move forward and get ahead in business?" I remember thinking, "Wow, how unique that perspective would be!" I wondered how different the answers would be when we asked men vs. women how women can succeed in business.

Our first man panel kicked off in February 2012. We focused that panel on the topic of how women sabotage their success in business from the man's perspective. We invited five male CEOs and executives from diverse industries and backgrounds to serve on our panel. We had one senior vice president from commercial banking, a CEO in commercial property management, the president of a public relations firm, one senior-level risk management consultant, and a retired admiral from the Navy.

·

We asked one of the panelists at the start of the event, "How do you feel about getting ready to share your perspective on what women do that sabotages their success in business?" His reply: "I'm delighted and petrified—all at the same time!"

Prior to our event, I got a call from one of our panelists, who said he had gone a little further than we had asked in preparation for the event. He told me he had reached out to his "brethren" and conducted a little survey of other high-level executives and male colleagues. My first question, "What was the response from your colleagues when you told them you were serving on a panel about how women sabotage their success in business?"

He said the responses were a mix of shock and awe. One technology executive reportedly said, "Are you crazy, going on a panel with all women and sharing that kind of information?" Another response from a high-level senior executive: "Dude, it takes a strong man to share the real deal, the real scoop with women." Still others wondered if he should strap on a protective vest and hard hat for the tomatoes that might be thrown his way.

Over 125 women attended our first man panel. As the moderator, I was fascinated by the opinions and insights our male panelists shared. Afterward, I asked a few attendees what they thought of the program and panelists. Many women said they were shocked by how candid the conversations were, and how authentic and spot-on the suggestions and ideas were. I overheard one attendee say to another woman, "I wish I would have heard this kind of candid advice 15 years ago. I would have done so many things differently in my career."

That first man panel was the catalyst for me to begin the process of interviewing men to uncover more on how women sabotage their success in business. I am no Ph.D. or researcher. I am, however, a curious and intrigued woman leader who wonders what we, as women, are lacking in order to advance in business more strategically.

Why a Man's Perspective is Important

I believe it's important to hear the perspective men have on this topic. Men are still in the power positions in business and industry. They still hold the major share of power and influence in Fortune 500 firms, along with 90 percent of boardroom positions.

Make no mistake. I want to see women advance in business and industry. I want to see women in corporate power positions. I hope to see higher percentages of women on boards and in the boardroom. The current and sad statistics for women give me pause and force me to ask, "Why?" What are we, as women, missing that keeps us from getting ahead? What are we not seeing that, if changed, might be the key to advancement?

Why Interview Men

To my knowledge, no one has ever asked men what they think women do that holds them back from advancing in business. Most business books for women are written by other women. I've read some fabulous books about women who have overcome great obstacles and women who have shared their leadership journey to greatness. I've read books by women who interviewed other successful women on how they climbed their way to senior-level positions. The question that continued to consume me was, "Has anyone ever asked men what women should do differently?" My quest turned into a process of interviewing men in senior-level positions and seeking their authentic answers, opinions and advice on how women can advance in business. My greatest challenge was to ensure that the answers were authentic, and to be given real advice and insight.

Should We Do as Men Say?

As you read this book, I'm not suggesting you do everything men suggest we do. It's the perspective men provide on how to advance that's critical. It's up to you to select the areas that will best help you advance in business. Some of the suggestions will apply to you. Others, not so much. Whether you think the message hits or misses the mark, I do hope the insights strike a nerve. I hope this book and the ideas presented create discussion, conversations and debate over what women should or should not do to advance in business.

Remember, I'm a woman too. I also want to lead, achieve and succeed in business. I want to advance, just like you do. It's in support of women that I sought advice from men. The information in this book is neither right nor wrong. It just is. Use or don't use the advice given, as it's entirely up to you. The information shared was provided from the unique perspective men have that women don't—yet.

Approaching Men to Interview

After our first man panel, I approached executives and CEOs I knew in the business community and started asking if I could interview them for a book on how women can advance more strategically in business. I reached out on LinkedIn and made connections to interview senior executives from diverse businesses and professions. I called companies with recognizable names and spoke to public affairs departments and "peeps" of senior executives—who thought I was a doing these interviews as a joke. More often than not, I received return calls back, if for no reason other than curiosity, based on the focus and subject matter. Some men thought I was absolutely crazy. Others were intrigued and agreed to be interviewed, but didn't want their names used in the book. Some executives flat-out refused to be interviewed. I even had one CEO for a national oil company laugh as he said, "Why the hell would I want to tell you how women can get ahead in business?" The great news is, hundreds of men welcomed the offer to be interviewed and were intrigued that women might want to hear their perspective on how to advance.

The Process of Interviewing Men

I started interviewing men in 2012. At first, I started with long interviews and conversations asking men what women should do differently to advance in business. I had lunch meetings, coffee meetings, appointments in corporate offices, phone calls by appointment, and email correspondence. In total, I conducted over 500 interviews and conversations with men. Some interviews were formal, and others were to get clarification on key points made by other

CEOs and executive leaders. I asked. Then I kept asking. It took me almost three years to complete all the interviews and find a nice cross-section from diverse businesses and industries. I also looked for men in a variety of roles, with a variety of duties and responsibilities.

Types of Men Interviewed

I interviewed CFOs, CEOs, CMOs, chief administrative officers, directors, senior executives, human resources directors, senior operations executives, floor managers, public relations officers, vice presidents, managers, and thought leaders. I even interviewed one retired admiral from the United States Navy. I interviewed men who were in their 20s, 30s, 40s, and 50s, and men in their late 60s and 70s. I was determined to interview men of varying ages to glean advice and opinions from different generations. I also made sure to seek advice and opinions from men of varying ethnic backgrounds. Diversity in age, position, role, ethnic background, duties and responsibilities was key to collecting a satisfactory range of viewpoints.

One thing that surprised me greatly was how many men whom I interviewed referred me to other men for interviews. I was amazed at how many introductions I got to other senior leaders in business, mostly because of their amusement that women might want to know the man's perspective on business and advancement. I took every introduction that was given. I had access to men I never imagined I could engage and interact with.

Why Men Agreed to Be Interviewed

On the front end, I thought men agreed to be interviewed because they were amused that women would want to hear their perspective on how to advance in business. Some men invited me in for the interview just to ask, "Why would women want to hear from us guys? Don't women feel we're the enemy keeping them from advancement?" Many men, however, answered two specific questions that gave me solid confirmation that their answers were authentic, real, and given with honesty. My qualifying questions were: 1. "What do you hope this book accomplishes for women to advance?" and 2. "Why did you agree to be interviewed for this book?"

I was pleasantly surprised by the answers. Many men said they wanted to contribute in a positive way, as they see how difficult advancement into senior roles and positions is for women. Others simply wanted to make a difference by sharing insights women otherwise might not hear through-out their careers. Still others wanted to give honest, practical, credible advice on how to get ahead. I knew these men were sharing from a good place and with great intentions to support women.

Then there were the interviews that touched my heart. More than 70 percent of my interviews were with men who expressed their concern about future generations. Many, many executives said they wanted to see their daughters and granddaughters have better opportunities in business than women have today. Men do see how difficult it is for women. The men who were most concerned about future generations are the ones I felt gave the best advice and rec-ommendations to advance.

The Women Men Respect the Most

Another question that led to an uplifting and inspiring answer was, "Who are the women you admire most?" I was surprised by the answer men gave most frequently. I thought the answers would be women from history or women in high-level executive and CEO positions in business and industry. The response I received to this question from over 82 percent of my interviewees was, "My wife" or "My mother."

When I asked them to explain why, many men told me how hard they remember their mothers working as they grew up or told stories of how their mothers worked two jobs or double shifts to get them through high school and then college. Many men described how much their mothers gave up to support them. And more men shared reflections of single mothers who worked and took care of the entire family on their own.

Men also recounted stories of the struggle their wives have as they strive to get ahead in business. I heard stories of how unfair the business world can be for women. These men know how difficult it is for women to advance.
In many cases, the men interviewed recognize that there is a continuing problem with women getting ahead in business. They know women have a difficult time. They know it's not fair, and they recommend you adapt—but without changing who you are. They also confirmed that for now, it's about women fitting into the male-dominated business world. But they say that is changing.

They also recognize many women are opting out of corporate America and starting businesses to fulfill what's missing from their careers and corporate positions. They see the pendulum swinging, albeit slowly, as more women advance into senior-level executive positions. They also acknowledged the sacrifices they see women make in lifestyle and family decisions.

Collectively, they suggested that to advance in business, women should modify their behavior and actions in the workplace and in business. It's not about changing you, it's about adapting to the business culture you are in for maximum results. As they shared their thoughts, I captured their ideas and opinions, and put them into this book. I hope you'll enjoy and benefit from their insight.

1

Deliver Results

"Take on every crappy assignment you can, and deliver great results."

According to men, we need to focus more on delivering results. Success is about doing work that produces results. It's not about working hard, working the longest, who puts in the most hours, who tries the hardest. It's about results. And it's about keeping track of your accomplishments, so you know what value you bring to the table.

Speak the Language of Results

Whether in units, dollars, percentages, increased productivity or performance, men said women need to speak the language of results. When you complete a project, note not just the accomplishment, but also how the project contributes to the organization. It's not enough to show you did the job; show how the project brings value through increased profits, productivity, performance, or saved time and money. One technology CEO said, "I remember one promising woman executive who showed potential as a rising star. She was smart, determined, and highly educated, but she didn't speak business. She was promoted into senior management when she learned to talk in terms of percentage increases in productivity and performance. She got attention at meetings when she shared how her department contributed to the bottom line in reduced expenditures. She started to speak results and share how she contributed to the bottom line. When she learned to speak the language of results, she advanced."

Keep a Scorecard

Men suggested women keep track of results, even small accomplishments. Log your achievements in a document or file. Keep track of numbers and percentages that show how you contribute to the bottom line.

A bottling distribution executive shared his perspective on keeping a scorecard of accomplishments: "I think every employee should learn to keep a file of accomplishments and achievements. One thing I hate the most is when review time comes around, and I'm the one to calculate what the employee has accomplished for the year. It's your job to keep track of your accomplishments and let me know at performance review time."

Another executive in the telecom industry offered some observations about converting your accomplishments into quantifiable results. "When you complete a project," he said, "look at the end result and make some calculations (or assumptions) for how you saved or made the company money. If you didn't drive revenue, then share how you improved the organization through the utilization of more efficient resources, which in my book equates to saving money. Saved expenditures are about as important as increased revenue. I think more women need to know this."

Take on High-Profile Assignments

Take on high-profile assignments that may not look easy and are an addition to your current list of duties and responsibilities. Many male executives said one way women can advance more effectively is to take on crappy assignments that lead to high visibility. As one business leader said, "While the project may look crappy and difficult on the front end, the benefit could be high visibility and exposure that showcases the fact that you can get results in spite of tough assignments." Another executive in finance said, "I look to promote those who can show achievement with the not-so-easy projects. When no one wants to take on a project, I look with favor on the person who chooses to perform it. Promotions don't always go to the person who skates by with the plum projects."

One executive vice president in banking told me, "I look at who's willing to go the extra mile. Someone who takes on a leadership role internally and volunteers within our organization tells me they are hungry to advance. It also leads to better exposure and visibility. I like initiative, drive and boldness."

"It's about sticking your neck out and taking on the tough project that gives you positive exposure to senior decision makers," said one advertising executive. The CEO of a mid-size catering company stated, "More women need to take on difficult projects. Get your hands dirty. I like to see women get in there and do the heavy lifting. There's more to catering than doing the pretty stuff. Take on the tough client, take the lead with a difficult project, and get in there and own the job."

Another hotel executive summed it up this way: "Women need to take on more responsibility and show results. It's not about working harder," he said. "The key differentiator? Show results," he advised. "The more you can show results and how you achieve results, the more arsenal you have for advancement."

Think Milestones

Sometimes, you have no control over how a project goes or how fast results are achieved. In cases like this, a few men suggested that you document even the smallest milestones as accomplishments. I used to be involved in numerous projects and "initiatives" in banking, and one thing I learned to do always was to log even the smallest milestones and achievements. As long as things advanced through milestones, benchmarks or decisions, I logged them. Even if a project is canceled or tweaked in a new way, you can still show accomplishments and results.

One executive shared with me that when a project tanked, he still documented how beneficial the effort was in saving future expenditures. As a senior leader in association management put it, "I realize the goals within our organization are hard to achieve. That's what goals are. I still need to see the end result."

A pharmaceutical VP said, "Let me see you produce. Trying doesn't cut it. I've worked with women who tell me they are working hard, but I say, show me results. At least show me what the results are that you did achieve as a portion of the goal." The key to success: Show results!

It's Never Fair

There is no fairness in business. Who rises to the top is sometimes not fair. According to a retired admiral from the United States Navy, "Business is messy, and it's complicated. It's never about fairness; so get over it. It is, however, about results." It's about who does the job well and can deliver results.

Solve the Problem

Many men said women need to be problem solvers and focus more on overcoming the issue or problem, as opposed to identifying the problem. One engineering executive observed, "I've worked with women who regularly bring problems and issues to the forefront at meetings, and identify things that need to be changed, modified, and improved. What I would rather hear, along with the problem or issue, is a recommendation of how to solve the problem or a recommended plan of attack. I see the problems; what I don't always have are the game plan and solution. Don't share the problem if you're not willing to recommend a solution. Solutions are about results. Give me that, and you're more valuable to the company as a result."

Seek Opportunities

Whatever your role or position, there's always an opportunity to show results. According to one HR director from an international technology company, "Our organization has numerous affinity groups, committees, and internal initiatives to get involved in. If you get involved with a committee, internal program or affinity group, show your involvement and activities as results. We have so few women in our organization, I'm constantly advising them to document their involvement and show the end results. Results may come from the most unlikely places. I once had a woman engineer I mentored, and we discussed how to use the affinity group she was involved in as achievement in results. We settled on how better employee attitude equals better performance, which leads to increased productivity. The end result is greater profits to the bottom line."

2

Know Your Worth

"It's either income, expense, profit, or loss. Business is about the bottom line. Don't detract from it."

One thing men were very clear about is that you need to know the worth and value you bring to your company and organization, and then articulate that worth. According to men, women don't seem to know or articulate their contribution in profits, revenue or the bottom line as much as they should. Here are a few things men suggested women should do to recognize and articulate their worth and value to their company and organization.

Dollars | Cents | Time | Efficiency | Costs | Value

Learn how to read financial statements. Know your worth in both dollars and cents, and your inherent value to the company. Do you save the company time? Do you increase productivity or efficiency of time and resources? Do you save the company money by reducing costs or expenses of some sort? Is there any kind of risk you help the company avoid based on what you do? What value does what you do on the job bring in benefits to the organization you work for? Know your worth. Learn to describe your worth in facts, statistics, percentages, dollars and cents.

Business is About the Bottom Line

No matter what department you work in or work for, there is a bottom line. You either make money or spend money in an organization. You either contribute to or take from an organization. The opportunities for advancement come when you know exactly what you do in your role and position, and how that brings value to the company. Even if you don't make money for an organization, your value might be bringing greater productivity to the bottom line. Any position can bring value; you need to find out how you can measure it in dollars, cents, time, percentages, saved resources or expenditures. This is where numbers and statistics rule!

Leverage Your Results

According to men, the reason results are so critical to advancement is that you have the opportunity to own your results, and strategically share and leverage the value. One senior manager in real estate observed that the beauty of results is how you can leverage your achievements to your advantage. "My advice to women is to self-promote at strategic times by sharing what you've accomplished in results that equal value. Speak in terms of your accomplishments. In a meeting? Want to showcase your results? Throw in a few well-chosen accomplishments and articulate how this supports the bottom line, and your street credit will immediately go up in the eyes of senior management. To them, it will be clear that you can produce results and are highly valuable to the company."

Another senior executive strongly suggested that women bring their list of accomplishments—shown as results—in value-based terms to every performance review. "Women need to be much more focused on showcasing their achievements and the value they bring to the company," he said. "It's not about doing a good job and working hard. Tell me what you accomplished in detail, and show me the value that brings to our organization."

A senior vice president in publishing said, "I recall one woman who showcased her achievements in dollars and cents in total each year at her executive review meeting. When we were looking for the right candidate to bring up to senior management, this one received the promotion. It was easy to see what value she brought to the table because she documented her worth in dollars and cents."

The CEO of an executive placement firm said, "I like to see percentages, dollars, accomplishments, and lots of numbers in resumes." A VP of technology noted, "When I'm looking for a strong candidate, I interview those who show hard facts and achievements on their resume in quantifiable terms. You've got to answer the burning question for me as to how you've achieved and produced value."

3

Turn Your Ask On

"If you don't ask, you don't get. Period."

In my interviews and discussions with men, they suggested women need to get better at asking for what they want in order to advance in business. Many men observed that you can't get what you don't ask for. A few slices of direct advice to women:

- "If you don't ask for more money, you won't get it."
- "If you don't ask for the next promotion, no one will know where you want to go in the company."
- "If you don't jockey and position yourself and ask for the highly visible projects, they will go to someone else."
- "If you keep quiet and don't ask for what you need to progress and advance, be happy with what you got."

Ouch. I'm in pain just writing this.

It's Only a Question

When you realize that asking for something can only be met with approval or denial, it takes away some of the threat of the ask. According to men, asking is only a question. It's not a statement or belief. What it does is force an answer. Conversation and discussion can result from a powerful question.

"I ask all the time in my profession," said one public relations executive. "I've had many, many women on our staff who turn and burn quickly from this profession because they can't quickly get comfortable asking.

"I advise women to see questions as a non-threatening way to get to quick answers. Once I hear no, my next question is to find out why. It tells me where the other party stands, and then the negotiations can begin."

Some men said women seem to put too much pressure on the ask, presenting it more as if it were a demand, command or threat. One VP of production put it this way: "I suggest women remember the following when they ask for more money for their department or unit. When you ask for more resources, it's a question, not a demand or threat. I understand the importance of telling me why you need it, but I don't like it when a request feels like it's fueled by anger. Just ask me the question, and be prepared to show objectively why the increased amount is needed and will benefit your department.

"The same goes for increases in salary or requests for a promotion. Ask me first, wait for my response, and then objectively present your reasons why. Also, share specifically how you are more valuable to the organization and how the company will benefit by dedicating more financial resources to you."

How to Ask

The key to asking and getting what you want is to leave the emotion out of the ask. According to men, the key is to ask with a "take it or leave it" mind-set. One pharmaceutical director shared the following story: "I observed one of the best maneuvers in a boardroom just last month. I watched one of our senior female directors put forth a question to the entire team in such a way that no one had any clue as to whether she was for or against the decision. I knew she was hoping for yes, but no one else around the table did. It was brilliant. Of course, she got the decision she was hoping for. The brilliance of the maneuver was in how she maintained absolute objectivity with no emotion when she posed the options and asked the question. I don't think she would have had the same outcome had she stated her case and position, where everyone knew which decision she was lobbying for."

No Means Not Now

To men, "no" means "not now." There is success in persistence. According to men, if you ask and the answer you get is no, follow up with, "Can you tell me the reason why? Can you tell me what would need to happen in order for the answer to be yes?" Across the board, men said women either don't ask in the first place or seem to give up after the first try. So ask! And then ask again.

"I have seen many women give up on the first no they receive," said one staffing agency CEO, "and I can tell you for a fact I wouldn't be where I am today in this role had I learned to accept no on the first response."

An executive in sports management added, "It's also important to be mindful when you're asking over and over for the same thing. Just because you hear no the first time doesn't mean you keep asking and asking and asking. Pick your time and pick your battle. Once you hear no, it's OK to ask why, but then retreat, revise your battle plan, and attack again at a later date."

See the Ask as a Starting Point

Another key point, men emphasize, is that no is just a starting point. One hospital administrator admitted, "I always say no just to get the key points out in the open. Why women don't get in the ring and ask a second or third time always puzzles me. I would advise that women understand that a no is simply a starting place for debate, discussion and negotiation."

Across the board, men emphasized that the ask is the start of the game. Once you hear the answer, you can follow up with questions that get to the heart of the matter, then tweak and revise your strategy—so ultimately, you can get what you want.

Be Specific in Your Ask

According to men, the "art of the ask" is to be specific. It's not enough to ask for a raise; request a specific amount or percentage. Then be ready with supporting results and evidence as to why you deserve the raise or promotion. Want to lead a project you feel you deserve? Set a meeting and ask for the project. Then provide facts and figures to explain why you are ready to take it on and deserve the project. But, men cautioned, be thrifty with words; don't provide more information than needed.

In one interview with a senior leader in the hotel industry, he shared the following story: "I remember one instance with one of our sales managers and she was asking for an increase in her expense budget. What I got was a rant on every justification known to the world as to why she needed the increase and how hard she worked with a limited budget. What she should have done is ask for the increase specifically and objectively define why on that one ask. Once I trudged through all the other reasons that she brought in to the conversation, I finally gave her a positive answer. It took me some diligence to get the request down to one key point."

When to Ask

Be strategic about when and where you ask. Men say that when you ask and where you ask are as important as being specific. Whether you ask in a one-to-one setting or in front of others can make a big difference in the response you receive. One vice president in the financial industry suggested that you ask in person, especially if the ask has anything to do with money or financial benefit. Another business leader suggested that meeting face-to-face should be your first choice and priority. One commercial printing VP stated, "You miss the nonverbal cues if you try to ask over the phone or via email. Skype is OK, too. However, I like to look 'em in the eye when I ask, so I can determine what they're thinking and how I'll react."

If you anticipate there may be questions or discussion about your ask, make sure you meet face-to-face. A phone call is second best.

Make it a Big Ask

Another tactic men shared is to always ask for more than you hope for. According to one mortgage executive, "I suggest women think about asking for more than what they expect on a first request. That way, you can come back with a lesser ask, which many times will be accepted, as the opponent feels they got a real deal. I don't see as many women do this as I see men do on my team."

Is This Your Final Offer?

According to men, women need to think about asking for salary increases, jobs, budget increases, staff increases, promotions or time off with the mind-set, "Is this your final offer?" According to men, women should make a habit of never accepting the first offer. Always ask for more.

Men say too many women view negotiation as a negative tactic, yet men see it as a standard practice in business to get what they want.

One computer IT owner shared the story of two managers who were pulling long hours for a merger and acquisition. One manager was female and one male.

Once the project was complete, the male manager showed up in the owner's office and asked for a compensation increase from the recent acquisition. When the owner responded with less than the male manager had requested, the male manager came back and asked whether anything else could be done to reward him for the time he dedicated to the projects and his efforts to complete the project ahead of deadline and under budget.

The female manager never made a request at all.

According to the IT owner, "I'll be darned if I didn't give them both a bonus. But if the male manager hadn't asked, and asked again, neither of them would have received anything."

A senior aerospace director told a similar story. "I see men who come in my office to ask for compensation or time off for additional projects or work served. I rarely see women come in and ask for compensation when they've completed an extra project. Men don't even question it. They come in and state their case."

The Power of Persistence

According to men, we need to keep asking. There is great power in persistence. According to one management consultant, "The one who gives in first, loses. Keep on. Keep with it. Keep asking."

4

Play the Game

"It's just a game, love.
It's just a game."

The simple fact is, men see business as a game. They're serious about business, but they view business as a strategy with a series of plays and maneuvers. It's like a game to be won or lost.

In my interviews with male executives and CEOs, they shared anecdotes of how business is like football, chess, Battleship, checkers, basketball, poker, baseball, golf, and soccer. Here are some viewpoints from men on how they see the "game" of business and their suggestions on how you can learn the "playbook" to advance more strategically.

Think Chess or Poker—Even if You Don't Play

Chess is based on a series of moves and plays, and you're always thinking ahead and strategizing. According to men, you should be thinking ahead to determine what your next actions will be. Think ahead about how you'll respond one way vs. another in an expected conflict. Think ahead about how you'll ask for something. Prepare. Think through your responses, and prepare in advance.

According to one executive in the building industry, "Women should be less reactive and more strategic in business. I always equate the game of business to poker. I look at my cards, see what I have, review what I need for a winning hand, and then decide whether I'm in or whether I'll fold. I choose my moves based on picking my next move carefully and strategically. I see women who bring emotions and feelings into business decisions. That's the wrong way to make your moves in business."

According to the CEO of an event management company, "Women should think of the end game before bringing up ideas they want accepted and approved by superiors, colleagues, and co-workers. Know what you want as the end game. It helps you decide on what move to make. That's how I make decisions about pushing forward or letting go."

There is No Losing – Only Winning and Learning

One male executive stated, "In business, there is no losing. There's only winning and learning." You will make mistakes. That's part of the process. Be willing to stretch yourself and do things you don't feel entirely comfortable with. Missteps are a heck of a lot easier to swallow if you view them as learning lessons, or what not to do next time.

Another analogy came from a franchise director. "I think women should look at business more like a football game," he said. "You always start the season thinking you'll be the winning team. You go through pre-season, and you have high expectations. Then you start the season. Sometimes you win and sometimes you lose the game. But, you always keep the prize in mind, the Super Bowl. That's what you shoot for.

"Even when you lose some games, which you might, you learn what worked and what didn't, and you get in there again to win the game. Test, try, and start all over again. It's not one and done.

"I worked with a woman who was one of our senior leaders, and she was great at her job and worked hard. However, she always beat herself up when she missed the mark with a client. While I was ready to discuss the next play, she was still licking her wounds over what she did wrong and apologizing. It's not how many times you fall down; it's how many times you get up afterward and try again."

Play to Win

Across the board men explained that business is competitive, and women need to view business from a competitive standpoint. As a senior vice president in the automotive industry stated, "You gotta play to win." According to men, women can't win in business if we don't play the game, and if we don't play to win. Games are competitive, and there are winners and losers. You only win if you get engaged and play.

One business broker said, "If I had one piece of advice for women, I would say you need to stop taking things in business so personally. Many times it's not even about you. It's about a decision that has nothing to do with you. And sometimes it's about me, and how I'm going to win and try to beat you. It's more of a competitive thing. Women should play to win. Leave emotion out. It's that simple."

One computer consultant observed, "Woman have a tendency to look at business too seriously. I think it's a gender thing here. I grew up playing sports, and I like to win. I like my team to win, too. I purposely put my daughter in team sports to be part of a team, to see what it's like, and help her understand the importance of winning, losing—and getting back in there the next day."

Know the Rules of the Game

No matter what game you play, there are rules. According to men, you need to know the rules of each game you're playing. In most companies, there is a strong culture for you to navigate, learn from and adapt to. The company culture is where you learn what the rules are. You find out what's OK vs. what's not OK. You see and observe what behavior is expected and tolerated. You either adapt and play within the culture, or not.

A senior principal from the insurance industry stated, "You need to observe, listen and pay close attention to what the rules are and how the game is played. Even different departments have different rules. Who's in charge and how they lead the team is one rule to observe. Second, how does the team interact? Are they serious and focused, or do they banter and cajole?

"You're either part of the team or not. I have worked with more than a few women who don't adapt to the team, or they view their own performance as the only measure of success in an organization. You're only as good as your team and its weakest link. You're either one of us or not. When the coach says, "Here's what we're going to do," you do it—or suffer the consequences. Then it's about deciding to stay or move on."

Take Risks

In games, sometimes you need to take risks and play to the outer boundaries. You won't win if you don't take chances, and that means some bold moves and taking on risk. According to men, women need to look at playing the game of business like the TV show Survivor. One leader in the title business said, "In Survivor, you won't be chosen if you play too nice. You gotta tick some people off once in a while. But then remember, to win the game, you have to rely on the team vote in the end. It comes down to outwit, out-win and outmaneuver your opponent." Another executive in the entertainment industry offered, "I think women should take on more risks. It's not about playing it safe and choosing the road already traveled. Sometimes you need to stick your neck out and bend the rules a bit.

"I remember one female producer on our team who stayed in the safe lane. She rarely took risks in recommending new themes for our lineup of entertainment. Our clients didn't like it. They wanted someone who would take on more risk and recommend an unchosen path. Once she started to play outside the lanes a little more and take on bigger risks with nontraditional themes, she excelled."

Learn to Bond and Build Rapport

Men said we should cajole and banter more effectively. It's about building relationships that will be valuable in the long term. Men also used the words "bonding and rapport" as key relationship strategies. According to men, you need to learn how to banter, which is the playful and friendly exchange of teasing remarks.

I know, you think I am nuts for presenting this strategy to you. However, I think it's good advice. Banter, done appropriately, is an effective way to build rapport. Have you ever watched men interact in business? They cajole and tease each other in fun exchanges and still get the job done. Ladies, according to men, it's a bonding thing. Take it or leave it, but I think it's spot on. Learn to banter—appropriately!

Pay Attention and Listen

Before you try this, pay attention and listen to how men banter among themselves. Handled inappropriately, this maneuver could backfire. Done well, you might create better relationships with your male colleagues.

5

Get Your Brag On

"Take the damn compliment!"

The truth, according to men, is that women don't self-promote when they need to. Many women struggle to avoid feeling braggadocios when they talk up their achievements and accomplishments. According to men, women need to take advantage of opportunities to self-promote their ongoing achievements and accomplishments.

"We" Should Be "I" From Time to Time

Yes, being a team player is an important element in business success. However, according to male executives, women don't bring out the "I" often enough. One president of a golf accessories company said, "I think women need to nix the 'we' and focus on 'me' more often." The president of a PR firm stated, "I see women who accomplish incredible tasks and take on projects that are difficult and near impossible to complete. When given recognition for their results, either publicly or one-on-one, these same women shrug their shoulders and tell me it was a team effort. To that I say, take the damn compliment!"

Take the Credit

Men agreed that women need to take credit for their efforts. When you receive a compliment for good work done, take it. "Don't sacrifice your efforts by saying what a great team effort it was, or how much other people put into the project. There are times, especially if you led the team, when you need to take the credit." Taking the credit doesn't diminish the people you lead. According to one chief creative officer from a design firm, "Leaders need to take credit.

Women will discount and circumvent a compliment like none other. I don't understand why they don't just take the credit and be done with it."

Pepper Conversations with Accomplishments

Another suggestion by men is that women should self-promote by strategically sharing their accomplishments and achievements. Especially when trying to persuade or influence, it makes sense to toss an accomplishment or achievement into the conversation. "Women need to throw in an achievement or two about their results when they're trying to get buy-in and engagement," said one chief financial officer. "I like it when I can hear about your achievements with specifics and end results. Tell me what you've done and how you accomplished the task."

When to Self-Promote

Another financial services VP said, "I see how much my wife struggles with self-promotion. What I've suggested to her is to pick the right times and key opportunities to share your successes. When my wife was looking for a promotion to a senior leadership position in banking, I told her that when she was in front of the people who matter—in other words, anyone who could help steer her career upward— she should point out a few of her achievements, just weave them into the conversation. She struggled with doing this at first, but after a few attempts, she got pretty good at pointing out her achievements when she was with those who mattered to her career."

Keep an Achievement File

Now's the time to pull out that log of milestones and accomplishments. We all have a tendency to forget some of our small accomplishments over the course of a year. If you log your achievements and accomplishments, you can share with superiors and executives when the time is right.

A managing partner of a law firm shared the following story: "I had a promising female attorney in our firm who refused to log her accomplishments, as I suggested each year during her annual review. Each time the female attorney's name came up for partner status, the partners asked for full details of what the attorney had accomplished and achieved. She did a good job. She billed acceptable hours. What was missing was all the other leadership efforts she gave both outside and inside the firm. While I had some details of the woman's accomplishments, damned if I could tell them all the details of her achievements and progress. As a result, a promising and accomplished attorney is still working at our firm and is not a partner because she refuses to understand how critical self-promotion and documenting her accomplishments are in order to make partner."

Humility Doesn't Get You Promoted

One finance director in the automotive industry said, "Humility is not a positive characteristic that gets you promoted. No one will, or can, promote you like you. If you seriously seek to advance in your profession, you must promote and announce your achievements. Women see it as bragging, men see this as a method to advancement. Keep track of your good deeds and achievements. Share as needed to get ahead."

6

Think Allies, Not Enemies

*"Ladies, you don't play well in
the sandbox with each other."*

In my interviews with men, a large number of male executives and CEOs said women don't support one another in business and in our professions the way we should. From the hundreds of interviews, conversations, and panel discussions I've been involved in, this is the top behavior that men feel sabotage our success in business.

I wish I could disagree with this. However, in my own commercial banking career, executive women did not truly support one another. In my interviews, men shared that we don't lift each other up in business. We're judgmental, territorial and too serious about our place, stature and pecking order. We have a scarcity vs. abundance mind-set. According to one male CEO, "Ladies, you don't play well in the sandbox with each other."

Support Other Women

Men suggested that we view other women as potential allies, rather than enemies. This alone would move the needle forward for women. A senior executive in the defense industry suggested, "Start by offering support to others. Offer to assist in some manner, or step in to support other senior women leaders. Give before you expect to receive. It all starts with one step of support. By the way, this is the same advice I would give to men as well." Another banking executive said, "You women don't support one another like you should. If you learn to help each other rise within the organization, everyone wins."

I also hear from omen in corporate positions who consistently share the challenges they face among women, who frequently treat one another as enemies. While some women do support each other for professional advancement, many don't. One senior executive in a national law firm said, "I can't understand why women won't support each other more. A year ago we had two partners in our San Francisco office. Both were women, and they were constantly at odds with each other. Among their male colleagues and partners, no problems. It was like watching children on a playground misbehaving badly. If the two of them had realized the collective results they could have harnessed together, magic might have happened. As it turned out, one moved to our Los Angeles office. I would have to think twice before having two female partners in the same office again. Really sad."

Even Madeleine Albright, former U.S. secretary of state, famously said, "There's a special place in hell for women who don't help other women." Isn't it about time we women stopped undermining each other and started thinking of other women as allies?"

What About Men Supporting Women?

One follow-up question I asked men was, "Why don't you support other women as much as you could?" And, "Why do you feel it's only women who should support other women? What about you? What about men supporting women more?"

I think I stumped a few men here. After an extended pause and silence, some men admitted that they don't know what to do. One male executive in a CPA firm told me he is a little fearful of what to do around women. He's worried about lawsuits, he's concerned with incorrect assumptions about a relationship centered on mentoring another woman, and he doesn't quite know what the reaction would be if he sought out women to support them. He did say he would consider a mentoring relationship if a woman asked him, but he doesn't feel comfortable seeking out the relationship himself.

One area abundantly clear from my interviews is that men do want to help, but they don't feel they can be proactive in this area. Many told me if a woman asked for their help or support, they would oblige. One executive in the retail industry said, "I never really feel like women want my suggestions or advice. In the retail business, I feel like I'm the enemy to executive women. I always feel as if I'm persona non grata to them. If a woman did come to me and ask for support or coaching or advice, I'd be happy to give it."

We're Back to the Ask

In my interviews, men said they look for women as well as men for coaching opportunities. However, they readily admit that men seem to have the "playbook" on how to ask for mentors and advice more than women do. Many executive men told me they would be happy to offer advice and counsel to women, but women don't ask the same way men do. As the principal in an engineering firm said, "I'd be happy to offer some advice to women, or even coach them, if they ever approached and asked. Damned if I can recall one single time when I was approached by a woman to be her mentor or advisor. I get requests from men all the time who seek my advice." The message, one more time: You must ask.

Change Is Slow

I believe things are changing, albeit slowly. Today, I see women looking for ways to support one another internally, within companies, and through conferences, workshops and through organizations focused on diversity and the advancement of women. I see women striving to give back more and actively offer assistance through mentoring and support of other women.

Lift as You Climb

What seems to be the "unspoken" mantra within the male culture is to lift others while you climb the corporate ladder. This is tough to write, as many men shared numerous stories and scenarios where they observed women who were petty and judgmental about other women. Not so much with men. According to one executive, "There seems to be an unspoken message among senior women leaders. I got here on my own, so you figure it out yourself. Rare is the offer of giving back or supporting other women." Men suggest that as you climb the ladder to higher positions, think about giving back to other women looking to advance as well. Give back by offering advice to junior achievers, and make a point of mentoring other women in junior roles.

Get Involved

According to men, we need to get more involved and engaged with clubs, internal affinity groups, and associations of influencers and women leaders in business. Learn, engage, and experience the advice of women who have navigated tough waters, and who have learned how to advance and achieve. Join trade associations or organizations that have a focus on learning, sharing, and advancement. Reach out to influencers and leaders within an organization, and request an "informational interview" to seek their perspective on industry information or advancement. Don't go it alone. One executive in the architectural industry said, "I don't know why women feel they need to go it alone to succeed. I wouldn't be where I am today without a few key mentors and industry colleagues who supported me along the way." Get involved, and learn from other influencers.

The Law of Reciprocity

There is another law about building allies that men shared in my interviews. It's the law that states when you give first, you get much in return. Start by building relationships where you offer to give first. Offer assistance to others, ask how you can support other women. Offer a hand of assistance to others and be a phenomenal resource.

To many men, this is "how to dig your well before you're thirsty." It's also called "you scratch my back and I'll scratch yours." Another common analogy by men: "quid pro quo." The concept is, when you need something from someone, it's too late to ask if you haven't built a solid relationship.

One media executive said, "I learned early in my career that success and advancement really is who you know, not what you know in business. I have worked with a variety of women who seem to think you can work hard and get ahead. Nothing is further from the truth. One of the key elements of advancement is knowing the right people and building strategic relationships throughout your career. Women would be much more successful if they built relationships with the right executives."

7

Learn to Draft

*"No man succeeds alone; why do
women feel they need to?"*

cross the board men think women try to go it alone, which is a huge disadvantage for advancement. Men said women need to learn how to draft, which is to adopt and learn from the successful behaviors of those already in leadership positions.

Learning to draft comes from stock car racing (yes, another sport). In stock car racing, drafting can only be accomplished with two or more cars. When the lead car rockets down the track, it pushes through the air and leaves a low-pressure wake behind it. The second car can slip into that airstream and reap the benefits of reduced drag. Taking advantage of the car in front allows for greater speed and better fuel efficiency.

Don't Go It Alone

Women should learn to draft by finding a mentor who provides advice and shares her wisdom on how to be a better leader. Finding a way to draft and learn from someone else means you don't have to figure out everything on your own. Learning to draft means selecting a person or group of people as mentors for a certain purpose. Learning to draft is about finding, following, and learning from the right leaders at the right time and for the right things. According to one executive, "It's much easier to follow others and learn from their mistakes. If you want a shortcut to success, find someone to follow, and learn from them." Hence, learn to draft."

It's Not About Placement

According to men, you need to search, find, and follow achievers and influencers you can learn from with a specific purpose in mind. It's not about being "placed" with a mentor or advisor. It's about going out and searching, finding, and requesting someone to be your mentor for a very specific reason and for very specific things.

Think Advocates – Not Mentors

According to men, mentors are great, but advocates are what you want. The advocate relationship takes time to flourish and, many times, starts out as a mentor relationship.

Advocates are much more powerful than mentors. An advocate will work to publicly support you, and recommend you, and endorse you. Mentors are passive. Advocates are proactive! Find an advocate. Find someone who is willing to support you and your mission to advance.

Search for Specific Skills and Talents

The way to find a great mentor and advocate is, first, to be clear about what you're looking for in the way of advice or counsel. What needs do you have? Are you looking for advice on technical details, career management, or something more specific? The more you can pinpoint the advice and information you're looking for, the better the relationship will be, both for you and the person you'd like to be your advocate.

I heard from quite a few men that the worst scenario is when someone approaches them to be a mentor, but the mentee has no idea what, specifically, she is looking for in terms of advice and information. Know what you want, and be specific.

Do an analysis of your strengths and development areas. What areas of your profession or business do you need the most assistance with? Make a list of where you need counsel, connections or advice, and search internally and externally for the person who will bring you value.

Multiple Mentors and Advocates

I personally had the pleasure of benefitting from multiple mentors and advocates over the years, so it makes sense that you might benefit from having different people offer you advice on different things. Look for professional advisors and mentors who exhibit or have experience in what you seek or lack. You have a much better chance of working successfully with a mentor whom you approach for help in a specific area, as well as having multiple mentors to draw upon.

Approaching a Mentor – Advocate

You may find a mixed reception in your ask for mentors and advocates. According to executives and CEOs, the more specific you can be, the better the advocate role will be. From the beginning, remember that your potential advocate is busy, and whether he or she agrees to be a mentor may have nothing to do with you. Your timing might be wrong, your chosen mentor has more on her plate than she has time to give, or you're not a great fit in chemistry and personality. The best approach, according to executives, is to make a phone call or send an introductory email with the request.

In your request, point out why you are approaching this individual, explain that you will respect his or her time, and that you would benefit greatly from the relationship. Share why you feel that person's talent and expertise might be helpful to you and for the advancement of your career. One executive told me that when he is unavailable to be an advocate due to other priorities, he refers requests to another colleague or key executive.

The Heavy Lifting is Up to You

Don't expect your mentor and advisor to do all the work. You do the heavy lifting. You set the agenda. You follow up. You report back on actions and results. Respect your mentor's time by setting clear expectations of what you seek, as well as being sensitive to time and meetings. Many executives said if a mentee is unprepared or unorganized in meeting deadlines and time commitments, or fails to follow through, it's over. So follow through when you ask for assistance and advice, by acting on the advice and reporting back!

Not Just Anyone Will Do

Finding the right mentors takes time and patience. CEOs and executives are busy; that's why they got to where they are! Do some research on the individual you seek a relationship with, then have a meeting or conversation to see if he or she is the right fit for you—and vice versa. Most executives want to give back to potential high-achievers.

The Dating Game

Executives I spoke to said they expect a courting period to get to know each other and determine whether the mentee/mentor relationship is good chemistry and a good fit. Consider looking outside your company or within your industry. Seek influencers and high achievers within your trade association for mentor and advisor roles. A mentor or advocate doesn't always have to come from inside your current company. One of my best mentors and advocates came from an entirely different company and industry.

8

Speaking Of…

"Sometimes, when a woman speaks, it sounds like nails on a chalkboard to me."

In all my interviews with men, none of the questions I asked elicited such an outpouring of opinion as when I asked how women can be heard, understood, and be more influential in business. Men said we should watch how we speak and come across in every business interaction. One executive stated, "Sometimes, the manner in which a woman speaks and how they come across are like nails on a chalkboard to me."

When You Speak

So many pieces and parts come into play when you want to be heard and understood in business. According to men, if you want to be heard, slow down your speech, lower your voice and reduce the number of words you use. Keep to one key point.

Want your ideas accepted more frequently? Don't be so excited about your ideas when you present them. Share your ideas without emotion in a more objective manner.

Feel like you're working too many extra hours and not getting recognition or time off? As noted in Chapter 3, "Turn Your Ask On," speak up about the great work you do, and ask for extra compensation. And don't complain unless you have a solution.

So many slices of advice!

How You Speak

According to one design firm president, "I would recommend when you want to be heard and understood to share your ideas as if it didn't matter whether they were accepted or not. Recently, I had a creative director feel her ideas weren't being heard in our strategy sessions. She came to me and felt there were problems with her male subordinates not accepting her creative ideas. I had been in a few of the meetings she referred to. I respected her enough to share a few points that I thought diminished her authority as a leader. I suggested she present her ideas and suggestions in a more objective manner. I also recommended she shorten her words, slow down her speech and lower her tone of voice a bit. She took my advice, and it worked. Her team seemed to accept her ideas more readily and hear her more effectively."

No Emotion

According to men, women can be seen as more influential if they leave emotion out. According to one senior manager in government, "Passion is great; emotion is not." You need to keep your emotion under wraps.

The Wrong Words

According to men, women select the wrong words when they want to communicate with power and influence. Words like, "Um," "Well, you know," or starting a sentence with "I know you're busy, but..." are all limiting phrases and words that diminish your power to communicate effectively. And don't say "I'm sorry" all the time.

Up Speak

Your vocal inflection, or the change in pitch or tone of voice you use in communication, speaks volumes. "Up speak," or ending a sentence with a question mark, is one way women limit their ability to be heard and understood. "Up speak" sounds like you're asking a question as opposed to making a statement of fact or opinion. According to one senior manager in construction, "I had to work with one of my female managers, who consistently ended each sentence with a question. When she would make a comment or share a point of fact, she would end the sentence or phrase with her voice going up at the end of her sentence as if it were a question. This really diminished her authority, throughout the company and with her team. She didn't even realize she was doing it."

Voice Inflection

When speaking or presenting, make your voice a bit lower and deeper than usual. Women speak at a higher decibel level, and therefore, according to men, are harder to hear. Also, slow down your speech if you want your ideas more readily heard and accepted. In addition, emphasize key words for clarity and purpose.

Talk Less, Say More

Women have a tendency to be wordy. The secret to success lies in thrift of language. If you stick with the facts, and keep the story and backstory brief, your relationships among colleagues will be more effective. One executive said, "I would rather have you pop by my office and state that you will see me tomorrow as opposed to telling me why you're leaving early and what you will be doing instead of working. I don't need to know you're heading out early to see your son play soccer. Just tell me what; I don't need to always know why."

Stick to One Point

One executive said that women have a tendency to hold everything in and then let go of everything all at once. When communicating in business, keep your focus to a single point or issue. Don't bring everything up at once. "I wish women would stick to one key point when they're bringing up solutions or problems," one biotech founder said. "Bring out an issue, and make a recommendation for a solution. One issue. One at a time."

9

Be Visible

*"I like to look...
but don't make me look."*

Men say women should be strategically visible, and always present and mindful about their reputation in business. As one senior executive said, "It takes time and patience to build a positive, stellar reputation—and literally minutes to crumble a great reputation down to kibble in one fell swoop." In other words, watch your actions and how you come across at all times. Be ever mindful of your behavior and actions in the workplace.

Don't Do Sexy

I am stepping into a minefield with this suggestion from men. According to one male executive in the hospitality industry, "I like to look, but don't make me look." He was referring to women's professional work attire. I have to admit, I really didn't want to have to tell women to dress the part to be taken seriously. However, I had numerous discussions with men on this subject alone.

According to men, women should dress in a manner that calls attention to your professional expertise and caliber as a professional woman. "Sexy doesn't sell with me, but it does get attention, and for all the wrong reasons," one executive said. It's OK to be feminine and friendly, but it's not OK to be sexual. There is a fine line between expressing your femininity and using your sexuality to get ahead. Know the difference.

Whether it's short skirts or showing cleavage, don't think sexuality is a method to persuade people to agree with you or promote you. Across the board, men agreed, if you want to be taken seriously as a female leader and professional, dress the way you would like to be perceived. Intention equals perception.

Walk the Halls

In my banking career, I was told by a very senior executive that I should "walk the halls of executives" on a regular rotation. In my interviews with men, they suggested that women need to be strategically visible among senior executives, and be seen in the right places and circumstances. One male executive shared, "I made a suggestion to one of my junior female officers to interact and engage with the directors as much as possible. I told her to come up with a reason for engagement and interaction with senior executives and directors.

"I watched and observed her path to greatness. When the top positions opened up, she was brought up as a candidate on many occasions, with the end result of numerous promotions to senior executive status. She had smarts as well, but I know the visibility helped tip the decision in her favor because the senior leaders felt as if they knew her." The message here: be seen and be visible where it counts in your organization.

How's Brand You?

When you think of building a stellar reputation, it's important for you to know how you are perceived within the company, community or organization you work for. One CEO stated, "Women should concern themselves with what they say, how they say it, and how they present themselves. Good or bad, everyone is making judgments and observations about you, and how you come across and appear in business." If you show up late or act less than engaged, people notice. If you appear not to care or be concerned with quality work, you will be judged on how you behave and show up. As one senior executive concluded, "In a nutshell, reputation— whether you like it or not—is how you are judged by how you engage and interact, how you come across, and how you behave."

Act As If

Men said if you want to be promoted and rise to the top, you need to act as if you already have the part and the executive role. How you behave comes into play here as well. Act like a leader, and be perceived as a leader. In one discussion and interview, a large company executive said, "I regularly observe and ask about the reputation of any potential candidate I'd like to promote. I observe them in meetings, among coworkers, staff, and vendors. Actions and reputation speak louder to me at times, even more than experience, degrees, and intentions."

Give Back

While women juggle work, family and households, executive men feel women also need to find a way to serve and give back if they want to advance in business. This is tough, as so many women I engage with will testify that they have no time available to volunteer. Taking on a leadership role and giving back in the community increases your visibility and exposure. One executive said, "Don't forget to showcase your achievement in how you're giving back. Make sure you document your leadership role with your superiors. Find a way to make your leadership known to those who make decisions about your future advancement. Don't be silent; make your leadership on a nonprofit board documented where it's needed."

Get on Board

One reason more women are not in the boardroom is due to visibility and exposure. According to men, women don't plan and prepare for a boardroom role. When more women realize that part of their career strategy is to be visible and intentional about serving a board role, more women will be asked to serve on boards. One senior executive in financial services said, "I'd like to see more women serve at the board level and as directors. The problem is, I don't know see many women who are board-ready." According to men, there is a process to being asked to serve on a board. It's also about knowing the right decision makers in high-level positions. An executive placement consultant once told me, "Women need to go where they flock." In other words, be visible at director-level groups and associations. Networking strategically is a key move to set yourself up for being asked to serve on a board.

Men agreed that more women can and will serve on corporate boards when they understand that they need to start by serving on a nonprofit board. Women also need to make it known that they want to serve as a board member and be willing to interact and engage with the executives who make board decisions. This is profoundly where "whom you know and how you engage with them" is a key strategy. I would recommend reading the book, *The Board Game: How Smart Women Become Corporate Directors* by Betsy Berkhemer-Credaire.

10

Just the Facts, Ma'am

*"Don't tell me why—just tell me
what and be done. Period."*

When asked how women should behave differently to achieve better business results, men said women need to stick with "just the facts." In my interviews, men shared stories and examples of how women stir up drama, assume with limited facts, are too emotional at times, and need to curb the gossip and water cooler conversation. I can almost feel the pushback I'll get after you read this statement. In full disclosure, the men I interviewed were not coming from a petty or inconsiderate place. Their suggestions and advice were centered on how you can adapt your behavior to achieve better results in business.

Just the Facts

More than a few men shared that women need to keep the story, the side story, and the backstory out of business conversations. One executive from a construction firm said, "One of our project managers would bring project scenarios to me and start with the pre-story, then the story that led up to the situation, and then the facts. I finally had her write down the list of items she wanted to present to me so as to be efficient with our time. This worked. My suggestion to women is to leave out all the fluff, and get straight to the point."

It's Show Business—Not Show Personal

"Women seem to forget that it's not about emotions," one CEO said. "It's business. Facts. Statistics. Results." Make sure you leave the emotion out of your decisions. "I only make decisions based on facts," stated one VP in hotel management. "I remind women and everyone on my team all the time that it's about show business, not show personal. Just stick with the facts when making decisions regarding staff, vendors, or situations.

"It doesn't matter how much you like the person, or how the vendor will feel if we have to tighten our budget or select another vendor. It doesn't matter whether you feel a certain way, if you'll hurt one person or another in decisions in business. It's about the facts." Rely on facts, information, and statistics—leave your feelings and emotions out of it. You're not in your profession or role to make friends. You're in business to get results.

Keep the Water Cooler Conversation to Yourself

Don't stir up gossip or drama in the workplace. The executives I interviewed said men get caught up in office drama and rumors almost as much as women do. For whatever reason, according to men, women have a reputation for stirring up gossip in the workplace far more than men do. The answer is to simply abstain from the water cooler conversation and office gossip. End it. Focus on business and results. One homebuilder put it this way: "You can be friendly, but when the conversation starts to turn to who is doing what, see yourself out of the conversation."

Don't Make it About You

One key point men made in my interviews was that women have a strong tendency to turn business decisions into a personal assessment on whether they did or did not perform well. One CEO said, "I once had a woman twist a decision that was made very objectively into a personal attack on her ability to do the job. I didn't even see it coming. For whatever reason, she took my decision of having someone else take on an extra unit she managed as a personal attack and that I didn't believe she could do the job. That was the furthest thing from the truth, and I explained that our company was restructuring departments and units for equal distribution of resources. Sadly, she lost out on more than one promotion as a result of her turning business decisions into a personal attack on her abilities."

No Jedi Mind Tricks

Don't assume. According to men, women have a strong tendency to make assumptions with limited facts and data. Feelings and emotions should be checked at the front door. Take time to understand a situation before making assumptions on behavior, and how people come across in verbal and nonverbal communication. According to one male executive, "I once observed a very competent woman executive mind read what other leaders were thinking around the boardroom simply by their behavior. This was painful to watch, in numerous meetings, as we were coming off a huge merger and acquisition with a competitor company. Every director had been working endless hours to make the acquisition happen, and it was sad to see this woman, with such talent, mind read based on her (incorrect) assumptions of how people were coming across in their mannerisms and behavior. She started to second-guess herself and, as a result, she was bypassed for a new position in the newly acquired organization."

There's No Crying in Baseball – and No Crying in Business

I had more than a few male executives say women should take advice from the movie A League of Their Own, where Tom Hanks shouts, "There's no crying in baseball!" According to men, women should not cry in business.

I remember one time in my corporate career that my tears flowed during a meeting with one of my male superiors. It is one of my most horrific memories. I tried to hold it together as I reported on a project that wasn't going very well. It was killing me not to deliver the goods, as I knew was expected of my department and branch. After that experience, I trained myself that no matter what the situation, there was no more crying in business for me. Men said crying is one of the worst things women can do to diminish their influence, authority, and power in business. Find a way to avoid tears.

I had another executive share a scenario where a woman executive got up from her seat in a meeting, saying she needed to leave and would be right back. She came back a few minutes later and, after the meeting, explained that she was so distraught by a decision to lay off employees in her department that she was unable to control her emotions. She chose to leave the meeting, albeit abruptly, to cry. "This," said the male executive, "was a much better maneuver than showing emotion, getting upset, or crying during the meeting."

"Suck it up and hold it together" is the advice from male executives. It's a tough road in business, and tough business decisions need to be made. Whether you make million-dollar decisions or manage millions of dollars in resources or people, your mission is never to let 'em see you sweat. "It's like poker," said one CEO. "Don't let people know what hand you have or what you're thinking. Don't share too much personally. You should have a very small circle of trusted colleagues and advisors whom you show your inner layer to."

11

Be You

"Be yourself. Everybody else is taken. People trust authentic people. If you are not you, you are not authentic."

A according to men, it's not about changing you or who you are to be more successful in business. It's about adapting and modifying your behavior to the culture and circumstances you encounter in business.

Adapt, Don't Change

One CEO from a biotech firm said, "Women seem to think they need to change who they are in exchange for success and advancement in business. Or think they need to be a man. Nothing is further from the truth. Be who you are. Be authentic. Diversity of thought and opinion creates success.

"You do, however, need to adapt. Success lies in adapting to circumstances and responses, not changing who you are."

Be a Mirror

One concept, according to men, is to mirror styles of behavior in order to advance in business. Mirroring is a known strategy of imitating someone else's patterns of behavior. The idea, as explained by a number of executives and sales leaders, is that you have a greater chance of building rapport with someone when you emulate them. One executive in the medical device industry said, "I think it's important to observe the behaviors and actions of senior leadership. Women would do well to mirror the behavior of other leaders. Anthony Robbins wrote the book on emulating success. Follow the leader and their behaviors."

One chief marketing officer from commercial banking advised, "Adopt the behavior styles of those in executive positions. When in Rome, do as the Romans do. If you see someone being aggressive, you need to adapt to their style. If you see someone being passive and non-confrontational, adapt that style as well. It's about adapting to that behavior, not changing who you are as a person. I've been in more than one situation where I'm in my uncomfortable zone, and yet I knew I had to adapt to get the job done. If you're dealing with a culture that's cutthroat, your choice is pretty clear. Adapt, or suffer the consequences."

Don't Be a Guy

In my interviews with men, most suggested you don't change or try to be a man. "Don't pretend you are a guy," said one senior executive in accounting. "You are a woman and special, just like guys are guys, and they are special. Be you. Be authentic." The key to advancement, according to men, is to find the unique balance between femininity and authenticity. According to men, again, it's about results. How you get to the end game is up to you. "Adapt to the circumstances temporarily, and then get back to being you," said one senior leader in event management.

Stay True to Your Values

You are as good as you think you are. Hold fast to the values that define who you are. Don't abandon your core values and identity. "If you veer from your core and value as a person, you lose your identity and center," stated one senior executive from construction. "Think about how to align yourself with the right company, with the values that meet your core purpose. Anything else is just a job and a paycheck. You gotta do what you gotta do, but we're on the planet for a limited time, so make your time count with a company that fits both you and your values."

Aim Big

Aim big, and aim high. In my interviews with men, they said women don't aim high enough. According to one CEO of a technology firm, "Women seem to be OK with good enough. Good enough is never high or big enough. So aim high. Reach high. Go for the stars. Anything else is just existing without purpose. We all want to make our mark. Find yours. What footprint do you want to make in this world? Is 'good enough' good enough?"

The Price of Perfection

So many women seem to think perfection is the name of the game. According to many executive men, women need to lose their focus on perfection. "It's never perfect, and it's never done," said one senior executive from the action sports industry. "For whatever reason, I see women who focus on perfection, as opposed to getting the job done and producing results. Sometimes done is better than perfect. It's all about test, try, tweak, and refine. That's how we move forward. It's never done. It's never perfect. Lose the focus on perfection, or you will lose your ever-lovin' mind."

Another senior executive described how often he sees women struggle to be the perfect this or that, and it throws them off-center from who they are as a person. "Perfection is smoke and mirrors. It's unattainable," he said. "Success lies in getting things done and showing results through other people. More women need to see that growth in business is about getting the job done by inspiring others to succeed and having them produce results. Refrain from doing everything yourself, and stop trying to be perfect."

Give Up Being Superwoman

According to men, being authentic is about giving up the concept of being Superwoman, and doing and having it all. "Success comes with choices," said one manufacturing CEO. "Give up trying to do everything and have everything. I wish I had super powers, but I don't. I've made tough choices, and they've come with consequences."

A real estate director said, "I am great at certain things and ho-hum at others. To compensate, I find others who excel where I don't. For whatever reason, women seem to take it hard when they can't do everything and be everything to everyone. It's exhausting. Give up the myth. Be you, and excel in something great. Let go of the rest."

My Final Thoughts

When Will the Lights Stay On?

A few months ago, I heard a female leader say, "I'll know when things are changing for women in corporate America when I walk into the executive washroom and the lights don't turn on as I walk through the door." It's a telling visual. We'll know when more women have made it to the top in business when the lights stay on consistently. Right now, unfortunately, there just aren't enough women leaders using executive washrooms.

Here's another question. When will your lights turn on? Did any of the suggestions and advice from this book flip the switch for you? Are you inspired? Are you upset by the comments and advice? Are you ready to have conversations and discussions on the ideas in this book?

Are you willing to modify your actions to advance more effectively? Are you going to be the change you want to see? Are you willing to adapt your behaviors to get better results? We all know the definition of insanity. "Doing the same thing over and over again and expecting different results." And, lest we forget, business is about results!

It really is up to you. What will you adapt and modify? Which behaviors will you change? My hope is that you'll take the advice from this book in the manner in which it was intended. Not to change you, or have you change who you are or your values. And certainly not for you to become a man. The ideas were meant to be a comprehensive convergence of thoughts and opinions men have on how women can advance in business. Their advice is not right. It's not wrong, either. Some of the information in this book may be harsh to hear. It is, however, absolutely centered on providing value to you as a professional woman who wants to get ahead.

Believe me, I had a tough time listening to the array of comments and advice shared by the men I interviewed. It was hard to hear their perspective on so many things I've done in my past that sabotaged my success. Whether you agree or disagree with the thoughts outlined in this book, note that the men who agreed to be interviewed shared very specific details and advice because they want future generations to advance. They were real and authentic in their advice (like they told you to be) because they, too, are concerned about the future for women. They know the politics of business is unfair. It's what we do by individual actions and behavior that will make a difference. As much as possible, it's a true perspective from men who, for now, continue to hold the power positions in business and industry.

So, are you ready to play the game? Ready to show results? Ready to get your brag on? Will you search for mentors and advocates? Do you know your worth? Are you willing to be visible and state just the facts? Are you ready to move forward and turn your ask on? And the biggest question of all: Are you willing to support other women in their advancement and success? I hope so! To that I say, "Go get 'em!"

About the Author

Michelle Bergquist is a nationally recognized author, award-winning entrepreneur, lively moderator and engaging, professional speaker.

Currently, Michelle is the CEO and Co-Founder of Connected Women of Influence, a leading powerhouse community of b2b women owners, executives and professionals who converge and engage to build high-performing professional relationships among like-focused peers in business.

Michelle is a passionate advocate for women in business by designing platforms, programs, connections and collaborative opportunities for professional women to lead, achieve and advance in business. In 2014, Michelle was recognized by the National Association of Women Business Owners as the Women's Advocate of the Year.

Michelle is the author of How to Build a Million Dollar Database, a business book that quickly became the go-to resource on how to build a powerful database full of priceless connections.

Michelle's professional background includes over 20 years' expertise in helping companies develop winning business plans, obtain funding, increase sales and improve business performance and success.

Michelle is a graduate of the University of Nebraska-Lincoln (Go Big Red!!) and a past board member of the National Association of Women Business Owners, the Fountain Valley Chamber of Commerce, YWCA of San Diego and the American Institute of Banking.

Michelle regularly speaks for a variety of business leaders, associations, groups, clubs and organizations.

To contact Michelle:
www.michellebergquist.com

Connected Women of Influence

Connected Women of Influence (CWI) is:
A leading powerhouse community of b2b women owners, executives and professionals who converge and engage to build high-performing professional relationships among peers in business.

Our Mission:
To build a strong, professional community that fosters growth, support and collaboration through the development of high-performing professional relationships, alliances and partnerships among b2b women owners, executives and professionals.

Our Philosophy:
We believe that b2b professional women converging together with the sole purpose of supporting one another professionally leads to better advocacy on behalf of each other. Our philosophy is that professional support, advocacy, partnerships and alliances lead to better business opportunities, and better business opportunities lead to finding increased value, which results in phenomenal growth and business success!

Our Goal as an Association:
To build supreme advocates, champions, alliances and partnerships among b2b women who lead in business.

We Connect:
We strive to connect our members with other professional peers in a productive and professional environment to share business experiences, learn from each other and provide resources and opportunities among each other.

We Cultivate:
We aim to build a vast, professional network of high-performing peers who provide services or products to businesses and who understand the unique needs and dynamics of serving business, industry and government agencies.

We Collaborate:
Our goal is to collaborate with each other to build high-performing professional relationships that lead to partnerships, alliances and advocacy among b2b women who publicly support one another, endorse each other and bring value and opportunity to one another as supreme advocates in business.

For more information about
Connected Women of Influence:
www.connectedwomenofinfluence.com